T5-CVR-021

ANIMAL RIGHTS

ANIMAL EXPERIMENTATION

Jessie Alkire

Checkerboard Library

An Imprint of Abdo Publishing
abdopublishing.com

abdopublishing.com

Published by Abdo Publishing, a division of ABDO, PO Box 398166, Minneapolis, Minnesota 55439. Copyright © 2018 by Abdo Consulting Group, Inc. International copyrights reserved in all countries. No part of this book may be reproduced in any form without written permission from the publisher. Checkerboard Library™ is a trademark and logo of Abdo Publishing.

Printed in the United States of America, North Mankato, Minnesota
102017
012018

THIS BOOK CONTAINS
RECYCLED MATERIALS

Design: Christa Schneider, Mighty Media, Inc.
Production: Mighty Media, Inc.
Editor: Megan Borgert-Spaniol
Cover Photographs: Shutterstock
Interior Photographs: Alamy, p. 11; AP Images, pp. 13, 19, 23, 28 (bottom); iStockphoto, pp. 17, 25; Shreveport-Bossier Convention and Tourist Bureau/Flickr, p. 27; Shutterstock, pp. 4 (left, middle, right), 5, 14, 21, 22, 28 (top), 29 (left, middle, right); Wellcome Library, London, p. 7; Wikimedia Commons, p. 9

Publisher's Cataloging-in-Publication Data
Names: Alkire, Jessie, author.
Title: Animal experimentation / by Jessie Alkire.
Description: Minneapolis, Minnesota : Abdo Publishing, 2018. | Series: Animal rights |
    Includes online resources and index.
Identifiers: LCCN 2017944012 | ISBN 9781532112577 (lib.bdg.) | ISBN 9781532150296 (ebook)
Subjects: LCSH: Animal experimentation--Juvenile literature. | Animal rights movement--Juvenile literature. | Animal welfare--Juvenile literature.
Classification: DDC 179.4--dc23
LC record available at https://lccn.loc.gov/2017944012

CONTENTS

WHAT IS ANIMAL EXPERIMENTATION?

When was the last time you used a new shampoo? How about a new medicine? People buy new products every day. But first, these products must be tested for safety. One way to test products is by using animal experimentation.

Animal experimentation is the conducting of tests on living, non-human animals. Most experiments are done for medical, drug, and product research. Companies need to make sure their products are safe for humans to use. So, they test the substances on animals. Animals often react to products the same way humans would.

More than 100 million animals are experimented on every year. Among them are mice, rabbits, cats, and dogs. Animals such as mice and rats are often bred for laboratory testing. Cats and dogs sometimes come from shelters. Other lab animals, such as chimpanzees, are taken from the wild.

Animal experimentation is **controversial**. Animals can suffer and even die from it. But these tests can help scientists find vaccines, treatments, and cures for diseases. The tests help humans stay safe.

ANCIENT EXPERIMENTS

Animal experimentation has existed since ancient times. Greek scientists and doctors began recording their experiments on live animals around 300 BCE. These animal experiments helped the scientists learn about the human body. This is because humans and animals have similar body parts.

Four hundred years later, Greek doctor Galen was studying the heart and blood vessels. He conducted his research on animals. Galen also wrote a book about how to experiment on animals.

Animal experimentation continued for the next several centuries. Scientists often performed their experiments in front of crowds. Some used live animals to teach students or the public about the structure of the body. In the 1200s CE, Spanish doctor

Galen was considered a leading authority in medical theory well beyond his lifetime.

Ibn Zuhr performed **surgery** on animals. This was a way to practice before performing surgeries on humans.

In these early experiments, **anesthetics** had not yet been invented. The animals often experienced severe pain. However, the practice was not highly **controversial** at the time. It was widely believed that animals existed to serve humans. Animal well-being was not a major concern.

RISE OF EXPERIMENTATION

Animal experimentation became more common in the 1900s. Before this time, products could be sold without any testing or regulations. This resulted in human injury and even death.

In 1937, a US company created a medicine called Elixir Sulfanilamide. It was made to treat sore throats. But the medicine contained diethylene glycol, a chemical that is poisonous to humans. It caused more than 100 deaths. Many beauty products, such as mascara and hair dye, also caused injuries at the time. Use of these products resulted in rashes, blisters, and even blindness.

The public demanded action from the US government. This led to the 1938 Federal Food, Drug, and Cosmetic Act. The law required companies to test drugs on animals before the drugs were sold. It also gave the Food and Drug Administration (FDA) power to regulate testing practices.

FDA researchers developed many animal testing methods. One researcher was John Draize. He came up with the Draize test in 1944. It determined how substances affected the skin and eyes. In the test, a substance is placed on the eyes or skin of an animal. Researchers then study and rate the severity of the animal's reaction to the substance. The Draize test became an industry standard for testing products that touch the skin or eyes.

Guinea pigs have been used in research for centuries. They are especially helpful in medical research because of their biological similarities to humans.

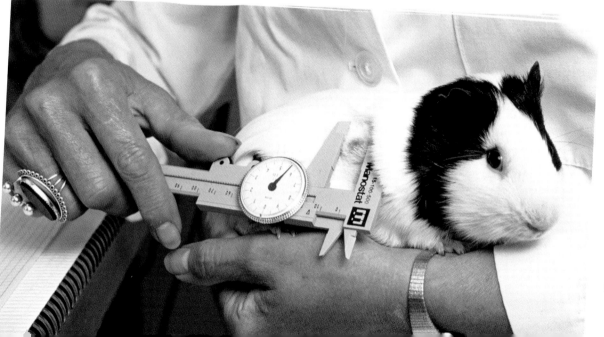

COSMETICS TESTING

The Draize test is still commonly used to test cosmetics, or beauty products, today. Cosmetics themselves aren't typically tested on animals. But these products' chemical ingredients are. These substances are tested on rabbits, rats, mice, and guinea pigs. This is because these animals breed quickly and are easy to handle.

Scientists conduct the Draize test on rabbits' skin and eyes. The rabbits are studied over a period of hours, days, or weeks. Reactions such as swelling, blisters, and blindness can occur.

Scientists also perform **toxicity** tests. For these tests, rats and mice are made to eat or breathe in chemicals. Researchers study the effects to determine which amounts of a chemical are harmful. The tests also determine if a chemical can cause **cancer**.

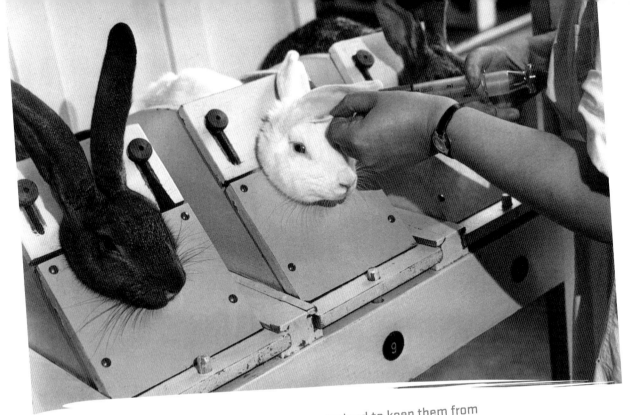

During testing, rabbits are often restrained to keep them from rubbing or scratching to relieve discomfort.

Animal experimentation in the cosmetics industry is **controversial**. Many researchers believe it does not correctly **predict** human reactions. For example, rabbits have thinner skin than humans. Also, their eyes do not produce tears as easily as human eyes do. Because of this, rabbits and humans won't always have the same reaction to the same chemical.

MEDICAL RESEARCH

Many scientists are against using animals for cosmetics testing. But most support animal experimentation for medical research. Animal testing has been a part of several scientific breakthroughs in the past 100 years.

In the 1900s, the United States experienced two major outbreaks of polio, a virus that affects the muscles. Each outbreak left thousands of people dead or **paralyzed**. Scientists studied the polio virus in rats, mice, and monkeys. Thanks to these efforts, a polio vaccine was created in the 1950s. By the 1980s, the United States was free of the virus.

Scientists developed the antibiotic penicillin in 1940. This was made possible by studying bacteria in mice. Penicillin has since saved millions of human lives by treating bacterial **infections**.

In 1954, surgeons performed the first successful human kidney **transplant**. The transplant was first tested on dogs. Scientists have also used animals to test treatments for high blood pressure. These treatments have reduced the occurrence of strokes, heart disease, and kidney disease in humans.

Some scientists argue these advancements could not have occurred without animal experimentation. Researchers continue to use animals to study **cancer** and other diseases. Their goal is to find better treatments and cures.

In the 1960s, dogs were hooked up to tubes that sent cigarette smoke into their lungs. Scientists used these studies to find a link between smoking and the lung disease emphysema.

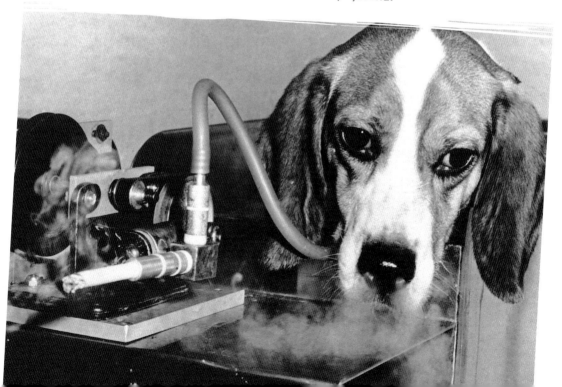

Despite many stages of animal testing, about 95 percent of drugs fail in clinical trials on humans.

Today, animal experimentation is most widely used in medical research. Many scientists believe animals are the most suitable subjects available for this research. Remember, this is because many animals are genetically similar to humans. They also have many of the same diseases and **infections**.

One type of medical research using animals is applied research. In this method, scientists have specific questions or problems to solve. They conduct experiments to answer these questions.

Applied research is often used in genetics and disease testing. Scientists add, change, or remove certain genes in animals. This causes the animals to develop specific diseases. Scientists study how the diseases develop. Then they can test different treatments.

Another common type of medical research done on animals is drug testing. Companies must follow laws to make sure their products are both safe and effective. Drugs go through many stages of animal testing before they can be tested on humans.

Metabolic tests examine how drugs are absorbed, processed, and released in an animal's body. **Toxicity** tests determine the safety of the drugs. **Efficacy** tests show whether the drugs work as they are supposed to.

EXPERIMENTATION ETHICS

Animal experimentation has helped save countless human lives. It has also improved the lives of animals as findings are applied to veterinary practices. However, it is still a **controversial** issue. Animal rights **advocates** believe animal testing is **unethical**.

Animals bred for experimentation often live indoors in cages. They don't get to interact with other animals. Some show signs of suffering or distress during tests. Many animals die because of testing. Others are **euthanized** after experiments are complete.

Animal advocates believe it is unfair to use animals for human gain. Some argue that all animal experimentation should be banned. Others believe that animal testing should be held to strict standards. This includes reducing animal pain and suffering in labs.

Because rabbits do not easily produce tears, they cannot quickly eliminate harmful or painful chemicals from their eyes.

Animal **advocates** are not the only people who argue against animal experimentation. Many scientists are against using animals for cosmetics testing. Some also raise concerns about using animals for medical research. Animal testing does not always correctly **predict** human reactions. Also, lab conditions and animal suffering might affect an experiment's results.

PROTESTING EXPERIMENTATION

Questions of **ethics** have sparked a growing movement against animal experimentation. Awareness of the practice first began to rise in the 1980s and 1990s. Photos and videos of animals in labs were revealed. Later, the Internet helped more people become aware of animal testing.

Many animal rights groups and organizations have formed to fight against animal testing. People for the Ethical Treatment of Animals (PETA) was founded in 1980. It is one of the largest animal rights organizations in the world.

PETA works to raise awareness of the ethics of animal experimentation. It does so with protests, undercover

In 1990, the University of California–Berkeley built a $14 million animal research facility. Hundreds of protesters marched across the campus in response.

images of labs, and more. It also publishes reports on animal experimentation and raises money for **alternative** testing methods.

Many other organizations have been established to inform consumers and stand up for animal rights. Groups often protest companies that use animal testing. Some protests have become violent. But most animal rights groups want to stop animal experimentation in a peaceful manner.

LAWS & REGULATIONS

One goal of animal rights groups is to help enforce laws and regulations that protect animals. The Animal Welfare Act (AWA) of 1966 regulates the treatment of certain animals in experiments. It sets limits on how many total animals can be used. It also limits how many times one animal can be used in experiments.

Animals protected by the AWA include cats, dogs, chimps, and rabbits. However, the AWA does not protect rats, mice, and birds bred for experimentation. This is because these are the most common animals used for testing. Lawmakers decided they were too numerous to protect. Animal rights organizations pressure lawmakers to amend the AWA to include these animals. They also fight for stricter regulation of laboratory practices.

Within the United States, individual states can pass their own laws concerning animal testing. California, New Jersey, and New York limit product testing on animals. Students in many US states can refuse to participate in science class experiments that use animals.

Outside the United States, other countries have stricter laws for animal experimentation. The United Kingdom, Germany, and several other countries ban animal testing in cosmetics. The United Kingdom also bans all testing on chimpanzees.

Animal rights are important to people across the world. In 2012, protesters in Italy marched against a facility that breeds dogs for research.

THE THREE Rs

Changing animal welfare laws can be a long and difficult process. But animal **advocates** and scientists continue to work toward improvements in animal testing. They focus on the Three Rs. These are replacement, reduction, and **refinement**. The Three Rs were first described by British researchers William Russell and Rex Burch in 1959.

Replacement means animals are no longer used for any type of testing. **Alternatives**, such as human volunteers, are used instead. But replacement is not always possible. So, researchers work to reduce the number of animals used.

Scientists also refine the methods used in animal experimentation. This may mean eliminating the animals' pain. It may also include improving living conditions in labs.

RIGHTS
SPOTLIGHT

BEAGLE FREEDOM PROJECT

Sixty thousand dogs are experimented on each year in the United States. Most of these dogs are beagles. Beagles are used because they are calm, trusting, and easy to handle.

The Beagle Freedom Project (BFP) is a program run by the nonprofit Animal Rescue, Media, and Education. The program began in 2010. BFP works to release beagles from experimentation. The beagles can then be adopted and live normal lives. BFP also works to connect labs with animal rescues. Animals used for research can find homes once research ends.

Dogs rescued from labs often behave like puppies in adult bodies. They are not trained or familiar with toys, furniture, or even the outdoors.

ANIMAL ALTERNATIVES

As science has advanced, so have animal testing **alternatives**. The United States and Europe approved the use of **synthetic** skin in the early 2000s. Synthetic skin imitates how real skin would react to certain chemicals. Scientists also perform tests on human cells. Researchers can use these methods to test the effects of drugs and other products on humans.

Another alternative to animal experimentation is the use of computer models. These models represent the human body and diseases. They can show how drugs affect the body. Computers are also used to study the makeup of substances. They tell how a substance will affect humans based on how similar it is to other substances.

Several US states have passed laws that require using nonanimal alternatives in research when available.

Finally, some studies can safely use human volunteers instead of animals. Microdosing is a method of testing a drug's safety and how the body processes it. Volunteers are given a very low dose of a drug. Researchers observe how the drug affects the volunteers' cells. The dose is too low to affect the whole body.

LOOKING AHEAD

The Three Rs have paved the way for many changes in animal experimentation. The National Institute of Health stopped testing on chimpanzees in 2015. The chimps used in medical research will be gradually retired to the federal **sanctuary** Chimp Haven.

Also, the number of animals used for testing is decreasing, especially in drug testing. This is because using human cells and tissues is now cheaper than using animals for drug testing. It is also more effective.

Lastly, more consumers are looking for cosmetics brands that do not test their products on animals. Many cosmetics companies are reducing or stopping animal experimentation. **Advocates** are working to create laws banning animal testing on cosmetics made in the United States.

Experts expect animal experimentation to decrease as **alternative** methods are further developed. However, most

Chimp Haven is in Louisiana. It opens to the public a few days a year on its Chimpanzee Discovery Days.

researchers think the practice will not stop completely. There are some types of research and experiments for which **alternatives** do not yet exist. This is particularly true in medical and disease research.

Animal experimentation has led to medical treatments that benefit both humans and animals. But science is improving all the time. Researchers continue to look for ways to replace, reduce, and **refine** animal experimentation in the future!

TiMELiNE

300 BCE — Greek scientists experiment on animals to help them understand the human body.

1200s — Ibn Zuhr performs surgery on animals for practice.

1938 — The Federal Food, Drug, and Cosmetic Act is passed.

1940s–1950s — The polio vaccine, penicillin, and other medical breakthroughs result from animal experimentation.

1944 — John Draize develops the Draize test. This becomes an industry standard for testing cosmetics.

1959 — William Russell and Rex Burch first describe the Three Rs. These are replace, reduce, and refine.

1966 — The Animal Welfare Act is passed in the United States.

1980 — Animal rights organization PETA is formed.

2010 — Beagle Freedom Project begins. It works to give beagles and other animals normal lives after experimentation.

BECOME AN ANIMAL ADVOCATE

Do you want to become an advocate for animal rights? Here are some steps you can take today!

Spread the word. Education is key! Tell your family and friends about animal experimentation.

Buy cruelty-free products. Avoid products that are tested on animals. You can usually find this information on a product's label or online.

Contact lawmakers. Contact your state's lawmakers and ask that laws protecting animals be improved.

Research organizations. Find an animal rights organization that is right for you. You can become a member, go to events, or sign up for newsletters!

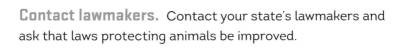

GLOSSARY

advocate – a person who defends or supports a cause.

alternative – a choice from among two or more things.

anesthetic – a drug that causes a person or animal to feel no physical pain.

cancer – any group of often deadly diseases marked by harmful changes in normal growth of cells. Cancer can destroy healthy tissues and organs.

controversial – relating to a discussion marked by strongly different views.

efficacy – the ability to produce a desired effect.

ethics – rules of moral conduct followed by a person or group. Something that is unethical is morally wrong.

euthanize – to kill an animal in a humane way.

infection – an unhealthy condition caused by something harmful, such as bacteria.

metabolic – relating to the process the body uses to turn substances into energy.

paralyze – to cause a loss of motion or feeling in a part of the body.

predict – to guess something ahead of time based on observation, experience, or reasoning.

refine – to improve or perfect by making small changes.

sanctuary – a refuge for wildlife where hunting is illegal.

surgery – the treating of sickness or injury by cutting into and repairing body parts.

synthetic – made by humans using a chemical process.

toxicity – the ability to harm or kill by poisonous substance.

transplant – the transfer of a body part from one individual to another.

ONLINE RESOURCES

Booklinks
NONFICTION
NETWORK
FREE! ONLINE NONFICTION RESOURCES

To learn more about animal experimentation, visit **abdobooklinks.com**. These links are routinely monitored and updated to provide the most current information available.

INDEX